HE ANIMAL FILES

WE NEED AFRICAN RHINOS

by Nancy Furstinger

FOCUS READERS

WWW.FOCUSREADERS.COM

Focus Readers is distributed by North Star Editions:
sales@northstareditions.com | 888-417-0195

Produced for Focus Readers by Red Line Editorial.

Content Consultant: Herman L. Mays Jr., PhD, Department of Biological Sciences, Marshall University

Photographs ©: Julian Parsons/iStockphoto, cover, 1; Stacey Ann Alberts/Shutterstock Images, 4–5; J. Natayo/Shutterstock Images, 7 (right); Simoneemanphotography/iStockphoto, 7 (left); Jonathan Pledger/Shutterstock Images, 9, 24–25; 1001slide/iStockphoto, 10–11; Red Line Editorial, 12; Simon Eeman/Shutterstock Images, 15; Yakov Oskanov/Shutterstock Images, 16–17; LouieLea/Shutterstock Images, 18; Daryl Balfour/Science Source, 20; Desrus Benedicte/SIPA/Newscom, 22–23; Sandra van der Steen/Shutterstock Images, 26; Lorimer Images/Shutterstock Images, 29

Library of Congress Cataloging-in-Publication Data
Library of Congress Cataloging-in-Publication Data is available on the Library of Congress website.

ISBN
978-1-64185-308-8 (hardcover)
978-1-64185-366-8 (paperback)
978-1-64185-482-5 (ebook pdf)
978-1-64185-424-5 (hosted ebook)

Printed in the United States of America
Mankato, MN
October, 2018

ABOUT THE AUTHOR

Nancy Furstinger is the author of nearly 100 books, including many on her favorite topic: animals! She has been a feature writer for a daily newspaper, a managing editor of trade and consumer magazines, and an editor at two children's book publishing houses. She shares her home with big dogs, house rabbits, and a chinchilla (all rescued).

TABLE OF CONTENTS

CHAPTER 1

BROWSERS AND GRAZERS

The hot sun beats down on a black rhino. The young male searches for water. His eyesight is poor. He uses his large nose to sniff out a water hole.

The rhino lies in the muddy water. He rolls around until he is covered in mud. The mud cools him off. It also protects the rhino's skin from insects and the sun.

A black rhino stops to drink at a water hole in Namibia.

Suddenly, another male rhino walks toward the water hole. The first rhino does not want to share his space. He lowers his head and charges the other rhino. The intruder flees.

Africa is home to two **species** of rhinos. Black rhinos live in South Africa, Kenya, Namibia, and Zimbabwe. They range across forests, **savannas**, and wetlands. White rhinos live mostly in South Africa. They roam throughout grasslands and savannas.

Despite their names, black rhinos and white rhinos both have gray bodies. To tell the two species apart, scientists look at the shape of the rhinos' lips.

The two species have different lips that are **adapted** for different diets.

The black rhino is a browser. Browsers eat leaves, twigs, and fruits. The black rhino has a pointed upper lip that helps it eat these foods.

BLACK AND WHITE

The white rhino is a grazer. Grazers eat mostly grass. The white rhino has a wide mouth and square upper lip. This shape helps the animal graze. At first, the white rhino was named for this mouth shape. But settlers mistook a word that meant "wide" for "white." Black rhinos likely got their name due to the mud they roll in.

White and black rhinos differ in size. The white rhino is the second-largest land mammal. The elephant is the largest. The white rhino can weigh up to 6,000 pounds (2,700 kg). The black rhino is smaller. It weighs up to 3,000 pounds (1,400 kg).

Rhinos are known for their horns. Females use their horns to protect their

Two white rhinos fight to defend their territory.

young. Males use their horns to fight rival rhinos. Both species have two horns.

A rhino's horns are made of keratin. This is the same protein that forms humans' hair. Rhino horns are hard and tough. They grow as much as 3 inches (7.6 cm) per year. If a horn breaks during a fight, it slowly grows back.

CHAPTER 2

KEYSTONE SPECIES

Black rhinos and white rhinos are important to **ecosystems** across Africa. They are keystone species. This means other species depend on them for survival. Rhinos have a large effect on their environment. Without rhinos, grassland ecosystems would suffer.

African rhinos share grasslands with animals such as zebras, giraffes, and elephants.

Thanks to rhinos, grasslands are home to a wide variety of plants and animals.

RHINO RANGES

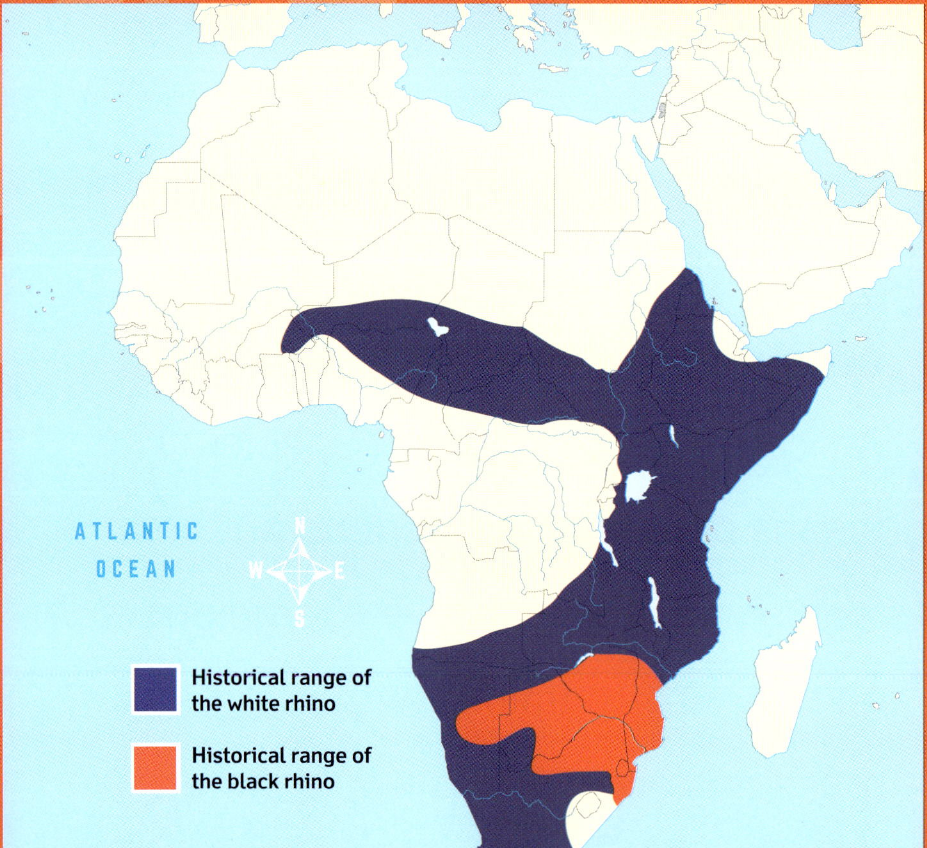

White rhinos are grazers, so they keep grasses short. Short grasses give other plants more room to grow. If rhinos went **extinct**, certain plants would not grow as well. This could threaten the other animals that depend on those plants.

Scientists studied how white rhinos shaped a national park in South Africa. Hunters had killed all the rhinos in the park in the late 1800s. But in the 1960s, **conservationists** brought rhinos back to the area. Decades later, scientists compared different parts of the park. Areas with many rhinos had more short grass cover. These areas supported a variety of animals.

Rhinos' waste also helps the grassland. That's because rhino waste is high in fiber. It adds nutrients to soil. The waste also contains seeds that the rhino ate. These seeds then grow into plants. They become food for other animals to eat.

RHINOS AND BIRDS

The disappearance of rhinos could affect many species. One is the red-billed oxpecker. This bird rides on rhinos' backs. As the oxpecker rides, it eats pests that live in the rhino's hide. Both animals benefit from the relationship. The bird is able to feed. And the rhino has fewer ticks. Rhinos help birds in other ways, too. When rhinos move through grasslands, they stir up insects. Some birds will follow the rhinos for a meal.

Red-billed oxpeckers rest on a white rhino.

CHAPTER 3

STRUGGLING TO SURVIVE

African rhinos face many threats. Black rhinos are critically endangered. That means they have a high risk of going extinct. In 2016, there were fewer than 5,500 black rhinos left in the world. White rhinos, on the other hand, are near threatened. That means they may have a risk of dying out in the near future.

Two black rhinos walk through a grassland.

White rhinos drink from a water hole on an animal reserve in Botswana.

The white rhino population is made up of two subspecies. Thanks to **reserves**, southern white rhinos are slowly rising in number. However, the northern white rhino is extinct in the wild.

Poachers pose the greatest threat to rhinos. These are people who hunt animals illegally. Poachers hunt African rhinos for their horns. Rhino horns are very valuable. In 2013, rhino horns were worth more than their weight in gold.

SAYING GOODBYE TO A SPECIES?

The world's last three northern white rhinos lived on a reserve in Kenya. Scientists hoped the one male would breed with the two females. But in 2018, the male died. Scientists plan to fertilize the females' eggs with sperm stored from males. Unfortunately, the two females are unable to carry calves. Instead, a southern white rhino will carry the calf.

The average front horn of an African rhino ranges from 20 to 35 inches (50 to 90 cm) long.

Poachers use guns to hunt rhinos. After shooting the rhinos, poachers saw off their horns. Other poachers use a drug to put the rhinos to sleep. Then they roughly remove the horns with an ax. When the rhinos wake up, they bleed to death.

Rhino horn can be ground into powder. Powdered rhino horn was once common in traditional Chinese medicine. For centuries, people thought rhino horn could cure many illnesses. Scientists disproved this belief. But some people still think rhino horn has healing abilities. Others keep rhino horns as trophies. They carve them into cups and other items.

Rhinos also face habitat loss. Humans clear land across Africa to build roads, villages, and farms. This activity destroys the plants and water holes that rhinos need to survive.

DOGS ON PATROL

A dog named Diego helps stop rhino poachers in Kenya. Diego and his handlers work at Ol Pejeta Conservancy. This reserve is home to the last northern white rhinos.

Diego is highly trained. When his handlers hear a gunshot, they unleash Diego. The dog runs up to 40 miles per hour (64 km/h). He uses his strong senses to find the poachers. He climbs cliffs, swims rivers, and jumps over fallen trees.

When Diego finds his target, he bites the poacher's arm. He holds the poacher until the handlers arrive. Then the handlers make their arrest. The program is so successful that handlers are training other dogs as well. The dogs will work on other reserves to keep rhinos safe.

A worker takes care of a white rhino at the Ol Pejeta Conservancy.

CHAPTER 4

PROTECTING RHINOS

People around the world are working to save African rhinos. They don't want the animals to go extinct. Without the help of humans, rhino numbers will fall.

Sanctuaries are safe, protected places where endangered animals can live. The Ngulia Rhino Sanctuary in Kenya is home to approximately 70 black rhinos.

A white rhino grazes in an open field in South Africa.

The Ngulia Rhino Sanctuary has been helping rhinos since 1986.

An electric fence keeps poachers out. Park rangers also use cameras to keep watch. When a camera spots a rhino, it takes a photo. If a camera takes a photo of poachers, the rangers give the photo to the police. That way, the police can arrest the poachers.

In 2014, the Thula Thula Rhino Orphanage opened in South Africa. This group raised rhino calves whose parents had been poached. Later, the group would return the calves to the wild. However, in 2017, two armed men broke into the orphanage. They killed two of the calves for their horns. After the attack, the orphanage closed. It could no longer keep the animals safe.

That same year, poachers also killed a rhino at a zoo in France. Afterward, a Czech zoo decided to dehorn its rhinos. The zoo hoped to keep poachers away.

If done right, dehorning is painless. Eventually, the rhinos' horns grow back.

One way to protect rhinos is through **tourism**. Rhinos are one of the "Big Five" animals that tourists hope to see on safaris. On safaris, tourists watch animals in their natural habitats. Safaris

FLYING RHINOS

In 2015, Rhinos Without Borders carried 100 black rhinos by plane. The group flew the rhinos from South Africa to Botswana. Botswana has the lowest poaching rate in Africa. The group also used a helicopter to carry rhinos. The rhinos dangled by their ankles for the 10-minute flight. They were then driven to a safe spot.

Tourists spot a white rhino on a safari in Kenya.

provide jobs to local people. They also bring in lots of money. As a result, safari companies are more likely to protect the animals. Safaris inspire tourists to protect rhinos as well.

FOCUS ON
AFRICAN RHINOS

Write your answers on a separate piece of paper.

1. Write a sentence that describes the main idea of Chapter 2.

2. What do you think is the best way to protect rhinos? Why?

3. Which physical trait gave the white rhino its name?

   A. its two horns
   B. its large size
   C. its wide mouth

4. What might happen if people stopped using powdered rhino horns as medicine?

   A. The number of rhinos would increase.
   B. The number of rhinos would decrease.
   C. The number of rhinos would stay the same.

Answer key on page 32.

GLOSSARY

adapted
Able to deal with a certain situation.

conservationists
People who protect plants and animals.

ecosystems
The collections of living things in different natural areas.

extinct
No longer living on Earth.

fertilize
To cause an egg or seed to start to develop into a new young animal or plant.

reserves
Areas of land that are protected to keep animals and plants safe.

savannas
Grasslands with few or no trees.

species
Groups of animals or plants that are similar.

tourism
When people visit an area for recreation.

TO LEARN MORE

BOOKS

Markle, Sandra. *The Great Rhino Rescue: Saving the Southern White Rhinos.* Minneapolis: Millbrook Press, 2019.

Marsico, Katie. *The Most Endangered Rhinos.* New York: Children's Press, 2017.

Newman, Patricia. *Zoo Scientists to the Rescue.* Minneapolis: Millbrook Press, 2018.

NOTE TO EDUCATORS

Visit **www.focusreaders.com** to find lesson plans, activities, links, and other resources related to this title.

INDEX

Answer Key: 1. Answers will vary; **2.** Answers will vary; **3.** C; **4.** A